50 WAYS TO GET YOUR CARTON

RECYCLE & CREATE MILK AND EGG CARTON CRAFTS THAT ROCK

by Ellen Warwick

STERLING INNOVATION
An imprint of Sterling Publishing Co., Inc.

New York / London
www.sterlingpublishing.com/kids

STERLING, the Sterling logo, STERLING INNOVATION, and the
Sterling Innovation logo are registered trademarks of Sterling
Publishing Co., Inc.

10 9 8 7 6 5 4 3 2 1

Published by Sterling Publishing Co., Inc.
387 Park Avenue South, New York, NY 10016
© 2010 by Sterling Publishing Co., Inc.

This book is partially comprised of materials from the following
Sterling Publishing Co., Inc. title:
Got Crafts?™ *25 Things To Do*™ *with a Milk Carton* by Ellen Warwick

Distributed in Canada by Sterling Publishing
c/o Canadian Manda Group, 165 Dufferin Street
Toronto, Ontario, Canada M6K 3H6

Distributed in the United Kingdom
by GMC Distribution Services
Castle Place, 166 High Street, Lewes,
East Sussex, England BN7 1XU

Distributed in Australia by
Capricorn Link (Australia) Pty. Ltd.
P.O. Box 704, Windsor, NSW 2756, Australia

Printed in China
Sterling ISBN 978-1-4027-5761-7

For information about custom editions, special sales, premium
and corporate purchases, please contact
Sterling Special Sales Department at 800-805-5489 or
specialsales@sterlingpublishing.com.

TABLE OF CONTENTS

INTRODUCTION

Who knew an ordinary egg carton could be so *egg-ceptional* or a milk carton could make so many *moo-velous* things. Instead of tossing them when they're empty, why not skip the recycling bin and reuse them instead? In the first half of this book, you'll see how egg cartons are a wacky, easy-to-cut shape that's just right for some cool and kooky crafting. The second half is all about milk cartons, which are handy containers that are strong, waterproof, and perfectly shaped for some fun and funky crafts. So get your *CartOn* with some easy-to-find craft supplies, a few household materials, and cartons you rescued from becoming rubbish!

Before You Start Crafting

Cartons are a snap to craft with, but there are a few tips and tricks to know before you get going on your first project.

Make sure the egg carton doesn't have any broken shells or egg goop in it. If it does, don't use that section of the carton.

Thoroughly wash the inside and outside of a milk carton before you start crafting. It can get pretty stinky inside if you don't! Make sure the carton is completely dry inside and out before you use it. If you're cutting open up the carton, dry it by opening the spout and placing it upside down to drip-dry over a sink.

Gather all the materials you need before you begin so they're handy when you need them.

Cover your work area with newspaper or a plastic tablecloth so you don't have a big mess to clean up when you're done!

For all of the projects in this book, cardboard egg cartons are the way to go. They're easy to work with and environmentally friendly!

Egg cartons all look alike, but once you get crafting you'll notice that they are all slightly different. Some have holes in the lids, some don't. For most of the projects in this book, any cardboard carton will do, but there are a couple crafts that require a carton with no holes in the lid.

We have used one-quart or half-gallon milk cartons in our projects. If these sizes are not available in your area, substitute a carton that is approximately one liter for the one-quart carton and one that is nearly two liters for the half-gallon carton.

Some milk cartons have plastic spouts with screw caps and some don't. Either kind of carton will work for any of the crafts. Just keep the screw cap on the carton. If you're painting the carton, paint the cap, too.

Any kind of paint works well on a cardboard egg carton, and metallic paints look *eggs-tra* awesome.

Only use acrylic craft paint when painting cartons. Because of the waxy outside coating, other paints, like tempera or poster paints, just won't stick.

Some cartons have more or darker markings on the outside, which means that you may have to apply a few coats of paint before they're all covered up—especially when you're using a light paint color. Be sure to let each coat dry before you start painting again.

For most of the projects, you can use either a glue gun or white craft glue. A glue gun is faster, but be *eggs-tra* careful because it's hot stuff! Make sure there's an adult handy to supervise. If you want to use white craft glue, you'll have to hold the parts together for a few minutes to make sure they stick.

To glue a carton spout closed, apply a thin layer of glue along the inside top edge of the spout with a glue gun. Pinch the spout closed and hold it in place for a few minutes while it dries.

When cutting a carton, you can use the carton's seams as guides. If you're using scissors, gently poke a small hole at the start of where you want to cut.

You can use a craft knife and ruler to cut open a carton, but make sure you ask permission from an adult first, and definitely keep the adult nearby to supervise. Wear a safety glove on the hand that is not holding the knife. Instead of applying a lot of pressure, make two or three gentle cuts to get through the carton.

When you need an egg cup for a project, that means you have to cut a cup out of the carton and trim around the edges like in the picture below.

When you're using the bottom of an egg carton, remove both the lid and the locking flap and trim the edges so they are smooth.

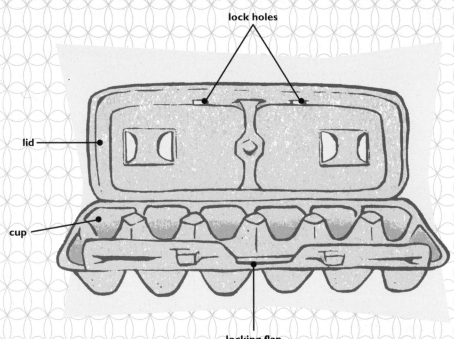

lock holes

lid

cup

locking flap

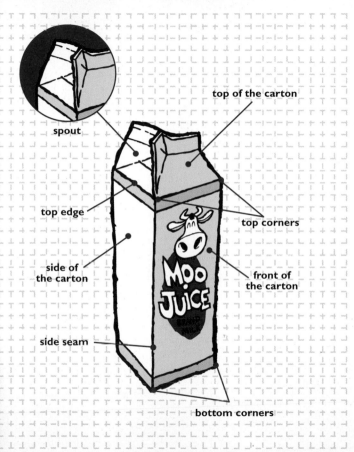

spout

top of the carton

top edge

top corners

side of the carton

front of the carton

side seam

bottom corners

Here's a guide to the different sections of cartons that you'll use in this book.

Now that you've got the scoop, it's time to get crafting. Just one more thing—don't worry if you don't have exactly the same paint colors or materials to work with that you see in the book. The craftiest thing about crafting is making it all your own style. Any way you *moo* it, it's sure to be *eggs-tremely* cool!

Fantastical Flower Fairy

This little fairy comes straight from the garden with her twirling tulip skirt.
Make one in every pretty color, and you'll be ready for a fairy party!

MATERIALS

A glue gun and glue sticks
1 one-inch wood ball knob or large bead
1 wooden clothespin
Craft paint
A paintbrush
Scissors
1 egg cup
6-inch x 6-inch (15-cm x 15-cm) piece of
  tulle or netting
1 pipe cleaner
Markers

1. Glue the wood knob to the closed end of the clothespin. These will form the head and the body. Let dry.

2. Paint the body and head. Let dry.

3. For the skirt, cut a hole in the bottom center of the egg cup, about ½ inch (1.25 cm) wide. Paint the skirt. Let dry. Slip the skirt onto the body and glue it on the inside to keep it in place.

4. For the wings, apply a dab of glue to the back of the fairy. Gather the tulle piece in the middle and lay it across the front of the fairy. Wrap the tulle ends around to the back of the fairy, crossing the ends and sticking them onto the glue. Add an extra dab of glue if needed. Let dry.

5. For the hair, cut the pipe cleaner into four even pieces. Bend each pipe cleaner piece into a U shape, and then bend the ends up a little. Apply a dab of glue to the top of the fairy's head. Stick the pipe cleaners in a row on top of her head. Let dry.

6. Draw on a face with the markers.

Gorgeous Glitter Flowers

Why wait for spring tulips when you can make these fabulous flowers any time of the year?
Add a touch of glitter, and these beautiful blooms will add pizzazz to any room.

MATERIALS

Scissors
1 egg cup
Craft paint
A paintbrush
Craft glue
Glitter
2 green pipe cleaners

1. Cut the wider egg cup edge in half to make two petals. Trim around the other two petal edges to smooth them out.

2. Paint the egg cup. Let dry.

3. Apply a little glue to the outside of each petal. Sprinkle some glitter onto the glue. Let dry.

4. Poke a small hole in the bottom of the egg cup.

5. For the stem, twist two pipe cleaners together, leaving about 3 inches (7.5 cm) apart at one end. Then, one at a time, wind each loose end around your finger to make a spiral.

6. Poke the twisted stem end through the hole in the inside of the flower and pull it down to the spirals.

BUNNY BOX

Tip the top off this adorable bunny and tuck your tiny treasures inside for safekeeping. What a cute way to store your fave earrings or your most glamorous ring!

MATERIALS

Pink craft paint
A paintbrush
2 egg cups
Scissors
Small pieces of light pink, dark pink,
    white, and gray felt
Craft glue
2 googly eyes
2 cotton balls

1. Paint the egg cups pink, inside and out. Let dry.

2. Cut two ears from light pink felt. Cut a round nose from gray felt. Then cut six thin whiskers from the white felt and a small, dark pink felt tongue.

3. Glue the felt pieces and googly eyes, as shown, on to one egg cup, with the open cup end down. Let dry.

4. Glue one cotton ball inside the second egg cup. Cut the other cotton ball in half and glue half to the back for the tail. Let dry.

5. Tuck something special inside the egg cup on top of the cotton, and place the bunny's head on top.

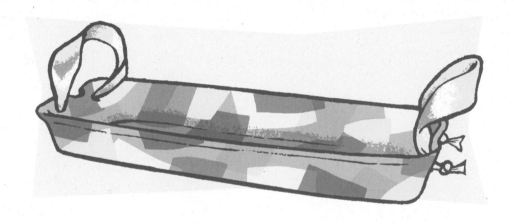

Décor Galore Tray

Add a dash of panache to your dresser or desk with this découpage tray.
A great way to store your desk doodads or beauty accessories,
this tray is as useful as it is pretty.

MATERIALS

An egg carton lid with no holes in it
White craft paint
A paintbrush
Tissue paper in a few colors
Craft glue
Scissors
¼ -yard (23-cm) of ribbon

1. Paint the egg carton top white, inside and out. Let dry.

2. Tear the tissue paper into small pieces, about 1 or 2 inches (2.5 or 5 cm) long.

3. Working on one section at a time, paint a thin layer of craft glue onto the carton top. Press a piece of tissue onto the glue and then apply another thin layer of glue on top. Continue adding tissue pieces, overlapping them as you go, until the tray is completely covered. Let dry.

4. Poke two holes into both of the short ends of the tray, about 2 inches (5 cm) apart.

5. Cut the ribbon in half. Poke the ends of one ribbon through the holes at one end of the tray and tie a knot at each ribbon end. Repeat to add a ribbon handle to the other side of the tray.

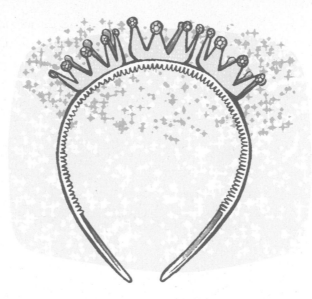

Twinkling Tiara

An ordinary plastic headband is transformed with a little gold paint and jewels.
A beautiful princess needs a tiara that's almost as dazzling as she is!

MATERIALS

Scissors
3 egg cups
Gold craft paint
A paintbrush
A glue gun and glue sticks
Small plastic jewels
A plastic headband

1. Cut a zigzag around the top of each egg cup as shown.

2. Paint each egg cup gold, inside and out. Let dry.

3. Apply a tiny dab of glue to the front of one point of one egg cup. Stick a jewel onto the glue. Let dry. Repeat to glue one jewel to every egg cup point.

4. Apply a generous dab of glue to the center top of the headband. Press one egg cup into the glue. Let dry. Repeat to add the other two egg cups to either side of the center cup.

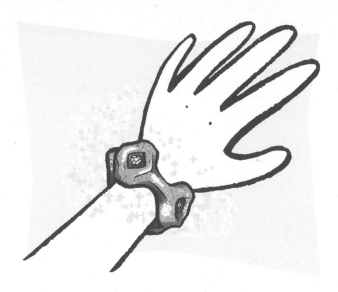

BEAUTIFUL BANGLE BRACELET

Wow your pals when you tell them that this bangle beauty is made from an ordinary old egg carton! Make a few in different colors and then pile them on for a funky fashion-forward look.

MATERIALS

Scissors
1 egg carton lid
A paper clip
Craft glue
Craft paint
A paintbrush
Clear plastic jewels

1. Cut out the middle section of the egg carton lid. Trim any rough edges.

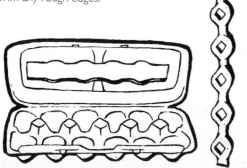

2. Run the carton piece under running water for a minute or two until you can bend it into a circle. Overlap the ends and slide a paper clip on to hold them together. Let the bracelet dry overnight.

3. Remove the paper clip. Apply a dab of glue to the ends and stick them together. Put the paper clip back on and let dry.

4. Paint the bracelet. Let dry. Then apply a coat of craft glue all over the bracelet to seal. Let dry.

5. Glue a plastic jewel into the center of each bracelet section. Let dry.

Dainty Blossom Dish

This pretty flower container is a perfect keeper of all your little bits and bobs.
A great way to keep your earrings, rings, or hair doodads organized.
This delightful dish will look lovely wherever you put it!

MATERIALS

Craft paint
A paintbrush
7 egg cups
A glue gun and glue sticks
Scissors

1. Paint each egg cup, inside and out, with a different color. Let dry.

2. Arrange six of the eggs cups around the seventh cup, spacing them evenly. One at a time, apply a dab of glue to the inside edge of an outside cup and stick it to the center cup. Let dry.

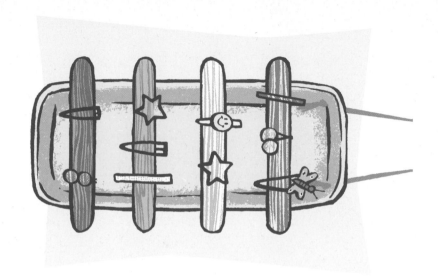

Hair Doodad Holder

You'll never have to frantically search for your favorite barrettes, bobbles, or hair clips again with this handy holder. Hang it on a door or dresser knob, or ask an adult to help you hang it on a wall. Wherever you put it, you'll be sure to find the perfect hair accessory whenever you need to do up your do!

MATERIALS

Craft paint
A paintbrush
An egg carton lid with no holes in it
Scissors
16-inch (40.5-cm) piece of ribbon or string
4 Popsicle sticks
A glue gun and glue sticks

1. Paint the inside and outside of the egg carton lid. Let dry.

2. Poke a hole at both corners of one short end of the lid. Thread a ribbon end into each hole and tie a knot inside the lid.

3. Paint the Popsicle sticks. Let dry.

4. Lay the lid down with the open side up. Arrange the Popsicle sticks evenly along the lid's edges. One at a time, glue the sticks to the lid's edges. Let dry.

Super School Bus

Load 'em up! This bus is road-ready and raring to go.
You can use pics from a magazine for the bus riders or a color-copy of your
class photo so you can have your best buds ride the bus with you.

MATERIALS

Yellow and black craft paint
A paintbrush
2 egg carton lids with holes
Small pictures clipped from a magazine
  or picture
A glue gun and glue sticks
Scissors
A drinking straw
4 egg cups
A pencil

1. Paint the outside of each carton lid yellow. Let dry.
2. The holes in the lid are the bus's windows. Stand
   the lid on its side, with the lock holes at the bottom,

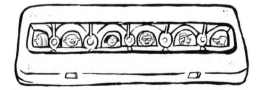

apply glue around the inside of one window hole. Press a picture into the glue so that the picture is centered when looking at the outside of the carton. Repeat for the other windows. Let dry.

3. Glue the two carton halves together with the lock holes at the bottom.

4. Cut two 3-inch (7.5-cm) drinking straw pieces. Insert one straw piece through a lock hole and pull it out the other side, so that the straw is sticking out evenly on each side. Repeat to insert the other straw piece through the other lock holes.

5. Cut off a little of the open end of the egg cups, so that the cups are about ½ inch (1.25 cm) high. Paint the cups black. Let dry.

6. Glue one egg cup to each straw end, as shown, holding them in place as they dry.

7. With the pencil, write the word *SCHOOL* along the top of the bus on each side. Then paint over the letters with black paint. Let dry.

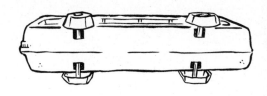

Beanbag Talent Toss

Test your tossing talent and rack up the points with this skill-testing beanbag game.
Each player gets three tosses, then add up the points to see who's the champ!
Test your skills even more by moving back one step with each new match.

MATERIALS

Scissors
An egg carton
A glue gun and glue sticks
Craft paint
A paintbrush
A marker
Three 2-inch x 4-inch (5-cm x 10-cm) pieces
of felt
About 2 tablespoons (1 oz) of dried beans, peas,
rice, or sand

1. Cut the lid and locking flap off the carton. Turn the carton over and glue the locking flap between the egg cups, as shown, so that the carton will be tilted up when you turn it over. Let dry.

2. Paint the carton. Let dry.

3. With the marker, write the numbers 1 through 12 in the bottom of the egg cups.

4. Apply glue along the two short edges and one long edge of one felt piece. Fold the felt in half to stick the glued edges together. Pour about 1 tablespoon (.5 oz) of beans inside and glue the opening shut. Let dry. Repeat to make two more beanbags.

FUN FORTUNE TELLER

Stuck on a problem? Not sure what to do? Let this funny fortune teller help you with your tough or not-so-tough dilemmas. Ask a question, roll the fortune teller, and see which message comes out on top. Whether or not you follow its advice is up to you!

MATERIALS

A glue gun and glue sticks
2 egg cups
White craft paint
A paintbrush
A marker

1. Apply a line of glue along the inside edge of one egg cup. Stick the other egg cup to the first one. Let dry.
2. Paint the fortune teller white. Let dry.

3. With the marker, write one of these messages on each side of the fortune teller:

Yes

No!

Go for it!

Forget it!

Think it over.

Why not?

Magnificent Medieval Castle

Put on your suit of armor and get ready for the joust!
All this castle needs is a dragon to fight and a damsel in distress.

MATERIALS

8 egg carton lids
A glue gun and glue sticks
16 egg cups
A ruler
A pencil
Scissors
Silver craft paint
A paintbrush
2 drinking straws
Construction paper

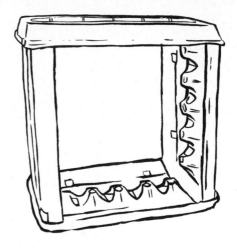

1. Lay down one egg carton lid. Apply a generous line of glue to the short end of another carton and stick it inside the short edge of the first carton so that it makes an L shape. Repeat to glue another carton inside the other short edge of the first carton so that it now makes a U shape. Let dry. Apply glue to the top edges of the U cartons and stick a fourth carton on top to make a square. Let dry. Repeat to make a second square.

2. Lay down one egg carton square flat and apply a line of glue around the top edges. Stick the other egg carton square on top. Let dry.

3. Glue five egg cups along the top edge of one side of the castle, starting and ending at each corner. Glue another five egg cups along the opposite top edge of the castle. Glue three egg cups to each remaining castle side. Let dry.

4. Measure, mark, and cut a 2-inch × 3-inch (5-cm × 7.5-cm) door at the center bottom of one carton.

5. Paint the castle silver. Let dry.

6. Cut the drinking straws in half. Cut four triangles from the construction paper. Glue one triangle to the top of each straw.

7. Poke a hole in the top of each corner egg cup. Poke one flag into each hole.

DUDLEY THE DEADLY DRAGON

This dragon may look friendly, but beware the sharp teeth! Be prepared to put on your armor and brandish your sharpest sword. But be careful—some dragons breathe fire!

MATERIALS

Scissors
2 three-cup egg cup sections
Red and green craft paint
A paintbrush
A glue gun and glue sticks
A pencil
Tracing paper
Green felt
2 googly eyes

1. Cut down the edges of each three-cup section so that they are even with the center pieces but are still attached.

2. Cut some pointy teeth into the edge of one end of each egg cup section.

3. Paint the inside of the teeth cups red. Let dry.

4. Apply a line of glue around the edges of one egg cup section, leaving the painted cup unglued. Stick the other cup section onto the glue, lining up the cup edges. Let dry.

5. Paint the dragon green. Let dry.

6. Trace the wing, foot, and ear templates with tracing paper. Cut out the shapes. Lay a shape onto green felt and trace around it. Cut out the felt shape. Repeat so that you have two wings, four feet, and two ears.

7. Glue one foot to each side of the body egg cups. Glue one wing to each side of the center body egg cup. Glue the ears to each side of the top of the head. Let dry. Glue a googly eye to each side of the dragon's face. Let dry.

It's Your Room Doorplate

Tell it like it is with this handy doorplate. Tag it with your name, your fave band, WELCOME or KEEP OUT, depending on your mood! And when you want to change the message, just wipe the board clean with a damp cloth and then with a dry cloth.

MATERIALS

Black non-washable craft paint
A paintbrush
An egg carton lid with no holes in it
30-inch (76-cm) piece of plastic lace
  or string
A piece of chalk
Scissors

1. Paint the outside of the egg carton lid black. Let dry.

2. Poke the plastic lace in through one lock hole and out through the other lock hole. Tie the two lace ends in a knot.

3. Draw a message on the board with chalk.

4. Ask an adult to help you hang the doorplate on a removable hook.

Asteroid Treasure Box

Add some outer space to your desktop with an asteroid that really rocks!
And inside is a secret hiding spot to stash your cash or other little treasures.

MATERIALS

Silver and black craft paint
A paintbrush
14 egg cups
A glue gun and glue sticks
Scissors

1. Paint the outside of the egg cups black. Let dry. Paint the inside of the egg cups silver. Let dry.

2. Place one cup black side up, add a dab of glue to the top, and then glue another egg cup on top with the silver side up.

3. Arrange five egg cups around the outside of the cups from step 2 so that the silver sides are out and the cups are evenly spaced at an angle. One at a time, glue the cups in place. Let dry.

4. Repeat steps 2 and 3 to make the other asteroid half.

5. Place one asteroid half with the center cup facing up, and place the other asteroid half on top with the center cup facing down.

DOGGONE IT DOG PUPPET

With a goofy grin and floppy ears, this faithful pal will always have lots to say.
Once you've made this adorable dog, it's easy to make other animal puppets—
simply change the paint color and the felt ears and tongue.

MATERIALS

A ruler
A pencil
An egg carton lid with no holes in it
Scissors
A glue gun and glue sticks
Brown craft paint
A paintbrush
1 small black pom-pom
2 googly eyes
1 piece each of light brown and pink felt

1. Measure and make a mark at the center of one long side of the lid. Measure the width of the lid's edge and make a mark that distance from each side of the center mark. Cut a line from the lid edge to the

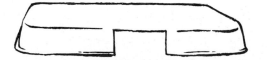

lid bottom at these two marks. Then cut along the lid bottom edge to remove this section of the carton. Repeat on the other side.

2. Gently fold the lid where you cut the first lines so that the two short ends meet. Apply a thin line of glue at the back edges and hold them together while they dry.

3. Gently make a fold at the center of the carton so the back ends meet.

4. Paint the inside and outside of the dog brown. Let dry. Now you have the dog's face.

5. Glue the pom-pom on to the front of the dog's face to make a nose. Glue the googly eyes above the nose. Let dry.

6. To make ears, cut two 2-inch × 4-inch (5-cm × 10-cm) pieces of light brown felt, rounding one short edge of each piece. Glue one ear to each side of the dog's head. Let dry.

7. To make a tongue, cut one 2-inch × 4-inch (5-cm × 10-cm) piece of pink felt, rounding one short edge. Glue the tongue inside the dog's mouth so that it is sticking out a bit. Let dry.

Carton of Eden Planter

You can grow a groovy garden in a basic egg carton. If veggies are your thing, start some peas, beans, or lettuce in the cups. And if you're a flower freak, try planting marigold, pansy, or daisy seeds. Once the shoots have come up, cut the cups apart and plant them—yep, the cups, too—in the garden or in a flowerpot. Be sure to use a cardboard carton, which will biodegrade in a short while.

MATERIALS

Scissors
A cardboard egg carton
A spoon
Potting soil
Seeds

1. Cut off the top of the cardboard egg carton. Then cut off the locking flap.

2. Use the spoon to fill each cup with soil, packing it down a little as you go. Place the planter into the egg carton lid.

3. Follow the directions on the seed packets for how deep you should plant the seeds. Plant about three seeds in each cup.

4. Lightly water the soil, then put the planter in a sunny place. Rotate the planter once a day and keep the soil slightly moist.

Fine Feathered Friends Feeder

Watch your flighty friends flock when you put this feeder in your yard or
outside your window. Keep the feeder filled and the birds will come back again and again.
They'll be your new BFFs (bird friends forever)!

1. Cut off the top of the egg carton. Then cut off the locking flap.

2. Poke a hole at each corner of the carton, about ½ inch (1.25 cm) below the top edge.

3. Cut two 36-inch (91.5-cm) pieces of plastic lace.

4. Poke one lace end through a hole and pull the lace through. Tie off the lace end so it can't pull back through the hole. Poke the other end of this lace through the opposite hole and tie another knot. Repeat to attach the other lace. The laces should cross in the middle.

5. Fill each cup with birdseed. Hang the feeder over a low branch or on a hook outside.

Buggin' Out

These bouncy bugs will brighten any day. With a grasshopper, a spider, a ladybug, and a butterfly, you're ready for any garden party. And when you're done, you could string them all up to make a bug-tastic mobile, too!

MATERIALS

Green, black, red, and yellow craft paint
A paintbrush
1 egg cup for each bug and a double cup
  for the butterfly
Googly eyes
Scissors
Green and black pipe cleaners
Black felt
Craft glue

For the grasshopper:

1. Paint the egg cup green. Let dry.

2. Glue two eyes to the front of the cup. Let dry.

3. For the antennae, cut two 1½-inch (4-cm) pieces of green pipe cleaner. Poke two small holes in the top front of the egg cup. Poke a pipe cleaner piece into each hole, and bend the top of each pipe cleaner over a little.

4. For the front legs, cut four 2-inch (5-cm) pieces of green pipe cleaner. Poke a small hole a little over from each eye. Poke two pipe cleaner pieces into each hole. Bend them down and then bend the ends into little feet.

5. For the back legs, cut two 3-inch (7.5-cm) pieces of green pipe cleaner. Poke a small hole on each side of the back of the grasshopper. Poke a pipe cleaner piece into each hole. Bend them down about 1 inch (2.5 cm) from the hole and then bend the ends into little feet.

For the spider:

1. Paint the egg cup black. Let dry.

2. Glue two eyes to the front of the cup. Let dry.

3. Cut eight 2-inch (5-cm) pieces of black pipe cleaner.

4. Poke four holes into each side of the spider, about a ⅓ inch (1 cm) apart. Poke one pipe cleaner piece into each hole. Bend each pipe cleaner down about 1 inch (2.5 cm) from the hole.

For the ladybug:

1. Paint the egg cup red. Let dry. Paint black spots onto the ladybug. Let dry.

2. Cut a small black felt circle and glue it to the front of the ladybug. Glue two eyes to the middle of the felt. Let dry.

3. For the antennae, cut two 1½-inch (4-cm) pieces of black pipe cleaner. Poke two small holes in the top front of the egg cup. Poke a pipe cleaner piece into each hole, and bend the top of each pipe cleaner over a little.

For the butterfly:

1. Paint the two-cup section yellow. Let dry.

2. Glue two eyes to the top front of one cup. Cut a small smile from the black felt and glue it under the eyes.

3. For the antennae, cut two 1½-inch (4-cm) pieces of green pipe cleaner. Poke two small holes in the top front of the egg cup. Poke a pipe cleaner piece into

each hole, and bend the top of each pipe cleaner over a little to make a small curl.

4. Cut two wings from the black felt, as shown. Cut a few small squares and circles to decorate the wings and glue them to the wings.

5. Lay the wings down faceup. Apply some glue to the back edges of the cups and press them down onto the wings. Let dry.

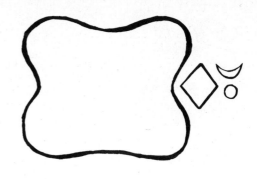

GOOFY GIGGLE GOGGLES

Spaz out with these spacey goggles and have some goofy fun. Then raid your costume box and stick on some silly stuff to go with it. Wacky or what?! Let the giggles begin!

MATERIALS

Scissors
2 egg cups
Craft paint
A paintbrush
Craft glue
Glitter
3 pipe cleaners
Thin elastic cord or string

1. Cut a ½-inch (1.25-cm) wide hole in the bottom center of each egg cup.

2. Paint the egg cups. Let dry.

3. Apply some glue around the holes and dip the cups in glitter. Let dry.

4. Cut each pipe cleaner in half. Wrap each pipe cleaner piece around your finger or the end of your paintbrush to make spirals.

5. Poke three holes in the top of each egg cup. Poke a pipe cleaner spiral into each hole. Bend the pipe cleaner ends flat inside the cups.

6. Poke a hole in each side of the cups as shown. Cut a 3-inch (7.5-cm) piece of elastic cord. Poke it through one egg cup hole and tie a knot inside. Poke the other cord end through a hole in the other egg cup, so that the cups are side by side and tie a knot inside. Cut an 18-inch (45.75-cm) piece of elastic cord and poke it through another egg cup hole and tie a knot inside. Poke the other cord end through the last hole and tie a knot inside. Put the goggles over your eyes and pull the cord over to the back of your head. Adjust the knots if the cord needs to be tighter or looser. Just make sure the goggles are not too tight!

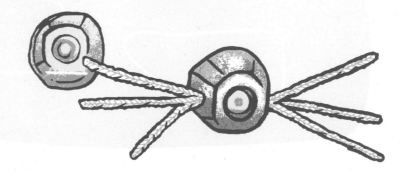

LITTLE MOUSE MASK AND EARS

Don't be surprised if you get a craving for cheese when you slip on
this cutie-pie mouse costume. Squeaking is optional!

MATERIALS

Gray and pink craft paint
A paintbrush
3 egg cups
Scissors
Thin elastic cord or string
2 white pipe cleaners

1. Paint the outside of the egg cups gray. Let dry.

2. Paint the inside of two egg cups pink for the ears. Paint a pink nose on the bottom center of the third egg cup. Let dry.

3. For the ears, poke a hole in each side of the ear cups as shown. Cut a 24-inch (61-cm) piece of elastic and string it through the holes. Put the ears on

your head and tie the cord at the nape of your neck.

4. For the nose, cut the pipe cleaners in half and then cut the pieces in half again. Poke a hole in each side of the nose and stick three pipe cleaner pieces in each hole for the whiskers.

5. Poke another hole on each side of the nose, closer to the edge than the whisker holes. Cut an 18-inch (45.75-cm) piece of elastic cord. Poke the ends of the cord through the holes and tie knots inside the nose. Try the nose on, and if the cord is too long, you can cut it shorter and retie the knot—just make sure it's not too tight!

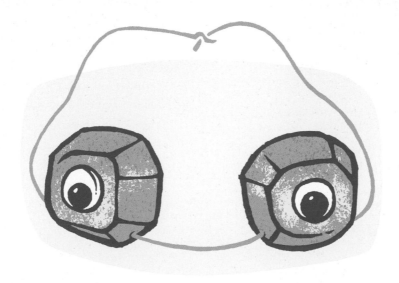

I'VE ONLY GOT (FROG) EYES FOR YOU

These ribbit-ing eyes will look frog-tastic with a green tee or sweater.

Hip-hop to the pond and croak your heart out!

MATERIALS

Green craft paint
A paintbrush
2 egg cups
Craft glue
2 googly eyes
Scissors
Thin elastic cord or string

1. Paint the outside of the egg cups green. Let dry.

2. Glue a googly eye to the bottom center of each cup. Let dry.

3. Poke a hole in each side of the cups as shown. Cut an 18-inch (45.75-cm) piece of elastic and string it through the holes. Put the eyes on your head and tie the cord at the nape of your neck.

Cha-Cha-Cha Maracas

You can shake it, baby, shake it, along with your fave band
with these musical maracas!

MATERIALS
(FOR TWO MARACAS)

About 2 teaspoons (10 ml) of dried beans or
  peas
4 egg cups
A glue gun and glue sticks
2 Popsicle sticks
A pencil
Craft paint
A paintbrush
Scissors

1. Put about 1 teaspoon (5 ml) of dried beans into
one egg cup.

2. Apply a dab of glue to opposite inside edges of the
egg cup. Place a Popsicle stick onto the glue so that
one end of the stick is just inside the egg cup edge.

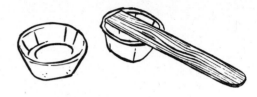

3. Apply a line of glue around the top edge of the egg
cup. Stick another egg cup on top and press to seal
the edges together.

4. Draw zigzag lines around the maraca top. Paint the
maraca in different colors following the zigzag lines.
Let dry.

5. Repeat to make a second maraca.

CHUBBY CHECKERS

What is there to play on a rainy day? Checkers! And it's even more fun
when you make the board and game pieces yourself. If you don't know the rules,
ask an adult, check online, or head to the library.

MATERIALS

Black and red craft paint
A paintbrush
24 egg cups
A pencil
A ruler
16-inch x 16-inch (40.5-cm x 40.5-cm) piece of
   cardboard or foamcore board
Scissors

1. Paint the outside of twelve of the egg cups red. Then paint the outside of the other twelve egg cups black. Let dry.

2. Starting at one corner, make a mark every 2 inches (5 cm) around the edge of the board. Draw lines connecting the marks across one way, and then across the other way, to make a checkerboard pattern.

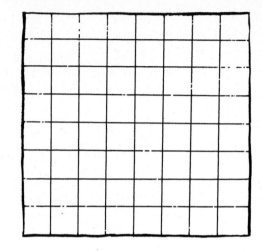

3. Paint every other square on the board black. Let dry.

UNDERWATER WONDER MOBILE

Create some ocean motion with this wild and wacky undersea mobile. Then, when you're hanging out in your room, you can tell everyone you've GONE FISHIN'!

MATERIALS

A glue gun and glue sticks
9 egg cups
Craft paint
A paintbrush
Scissors
Craft foam sheets
12 googly eyes
Thin ribbon or string
An egg carton lid
A ruler

For the fish (make three):

1. Apply a line of glue along the inside edge of one egg cup. Stick another egg cup to the first one. Let dry.
2. Paint the fish. Let dry.
3. Cut a top fin, bottom fin, and tail fin from craft foam. Glue the fins in place as shown.

4. Glue a googly eye to each side of the front of the fish.

For the jellyfish (make two):

1. Paint the outside of an egg cup. Let dry.
2. Cut a 2-inch × 4-inch (5-cm × 10-cm) piece of craft foam. Cut lines along one long edge, leaving about ½ inch (1.25 cm) uncut.
3. Apply glue to the inside bottom of the egg cup. Roll the craft foam piece up and stick the uncut edge into the glue. Let dry.
4. Glue two googly eyes to the front of the jellyfish. Let dry.

For the octopus (make one):

1. Paint an egg cup. Let dry.
2. Cut a ½-inch × 3-inch (1.25-cm × 7.5-cm) piece of craft foam and round one short edge. Repeat to make seven more tentacles.
3. Glue the tentacles to the inside of the egg cup, spacing them evenly. Let dry. Bend the tentacle ends up a little with your fingers.
4. Glue two googly eyes to the front of the octopus. Let dry.

For the mobile:

1. Cut six 18-inch (45.75-cm) pieces of ribbon.
2. Poke a hole in the top of each jellyfish and the octopus. Poke a ribbon end into each hole and tie a knot inside.

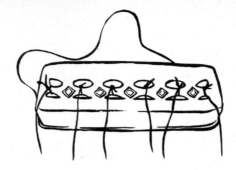

3. Poke a hole in the top fin of each fish. Poke a ribbon through the hole and tie the ribbon end in a knot.
4. Paint the egg carton lid. Let dry.
5. Poke each sea creature's ribbon end up through a hole in the egg carton lid, and then back down through another hole, as shown. Tie the ribbons so that the sea creatures hang at different lengths. Trim any long ribbon ends.
6. Punch a hole in each short end of the carton lid. Cut a 24-inch (61-cm) piece of ribbon. Poke each ribbon end through one hole and tie a knot.

WORTHY WALLET

Tuck your MOO-ney inside this easy-to-make wallet and you'll have a place to stash the cash you saved by making your own wallet. Follow the instructions below to make a basic wallet, and then customize it by adding pockets for coins, pics, or tix.

MATERIALS

A half-gallon milk carton
Duct tape
A self-adhesive Velcro® square
A ruler, a pencil, and scissors

1. Open the top of the milk carton. Cut down one side corner edge, then cut the carton bottom off along the bottom edges. Open the carton flat.

2. In several places across the carton, measure and mark 4 inches (10 cm) up from the bottom edge of the carton. Using a ruler, draw a line between the marks and cut along the line.

3. Measure and cut a piece of duct tape a little longer than the top edge of the carton piece.

4. Lay the tape piece down, sticky side up, and place the top edge of the carton along the tape, covering about half of the width of the tape. Fold the tape down over the carton edge. Trim the tape ends.

5. Fold the carton in half along the middle seam. Measure and cut a piece of duct tape a little longer than the folded carton piece. Repeat step 4 to fold the tape over the bottom edge of the carton piece.

6. Measure and cut a piece of duct tape a little longer than the open side edge. Repeat step 4 to stick the tape over this edge.

7. Stick one part of the Velcro® square to the center of the untaped edge of the wallet. Stick the other part of the Velcro® square to the center of the short taped edge, opposite. Fold the wallet in half and squeeze the Velcro® pieces together to keep the wallet closed.

LITTLE PINK PIGGY BANK

This little oinker is the perfect piggy place to save your pennies for a rainy day.
When you want to break the bank to buy something, simply slide the front
and back sections apart to get your dough.

MATERIALS

A half-gallon milk carton
A cardboard egg carton
Pink acrylic craft paint
A pink pipe cleaner
2 googly eyes
2-inch x 2-inch (5-cm x 5-cm)
  square of pink felt
A glue gun and glue sticks
A ruler, a pencil, scissors,
  and a paintbrush

1. Measure and mark 4 inches (10 cm) up from each bottom corner of the carton. Use a pencil and ruler to draw a line between the marks and cut along the line to make two pieces.

2. Fold the top of the carton flat and use a glue gun to stick it in place. Let it dry, holding it down as it dries if necessary.

3. On the top section of the carton, cut a line down the center of one side so it will fit inside the bottom section.

4. Cut out five individual egg cups from the egg carton. Trim the top edges of each cup so they are even. Glue one cup to the front of the bottom section of the carton to make a snout. This is the front of the piggy bank. For feet, glue two egg cups onto the bottom of each milk carton section, near the closed end.

5. Cut a small rectangle on the top of the front section of the bank, about 1 inch (2.5 cm) from the front edge.

6. Paint the entire bank pink and let dry. Repeat two or three times until the carton is completely covered.

7. Gently pinch the back section of the bank and tuck it into the front section. Slide them together so that about half of the back of the bank is inside the front section.

8. Cut a 4-inch (10-cm) piece of pipe cleaner. Wrap it around your finger to make a coil. Glue it to the back of the bank for a tail. Cut another 4-inch (10-cm) piece of pipe cleaner and bend it into a smile shape. Glue it to the front of the bank under the snout.

9. Glue the googly eyes above the snout.

10. Cut the felt square in half diagonally to make two triangles. Fold the two corners of the long edge of one triangle until they overlap and glue this edge to the top front of the bank to make one ear. Repeat to glue on the other ear.

Let's Go Bowling Game

Skip the trip to the bowling alley and create your own pins. You'll need to make ten pins, so why not make it a party? Invite nine friends over and you can each make one pin.
When they're dry, split into two teams and let the bowling begin!

MATERIALS

10 one-quart milk cartons
5 cupfuls of sand
Craft paint
A glue gun and glue sticks
A paintbrush
A ball for bowling

1. Pour half of a cupful of sand into each carton. Glue the spout openings shut.

2. Paint the cartons bright colors and let dry. Repeat two or three times until the cartons are completely covered.

3. Paint a number from one to ten on each pin.

4. Line up the pins in a triangle with one at the front, two behind that, then three, and then four at the back. Grab your ball and score one point for each pin you knock down.

COW CLOCK

An udderly adorable way to tell the time,
this cute cow will get you MOO-ving on schedule every day.

MATERIALS

A half-gallon milk carton
2 sheets of black felt
1 sheet of white felt
1 sheet of pink felt
2 large googly eyes
A clock works kit
A glue gun and glue sticks
A ruler, a pencil, scissors, a drinking glass,
   and a medium-tip black marker

1. Measure and mark 7 inches (18 cm) up from each bottom corner of the carton. Using a ruler, draw a line between the marks and cut along the line to remove the top. Turn the carton over so the open end is down.

2. Measure and cut black felt pieces to wrap around the front, sides, and back of the carton. Cut another piece of black felt to cover the top of the carton. Glue the felt pieces onto the carton.

3. Trace the widest edge of the drinking glass onto white felt and cut out the circle. With the black marker, draw the numbers 1 to 12 around the edge of the circle to make a clock face. Glue the circle to the lower part of the carton front with the number 12 at the top.

4. Poke a hole through the center of the white felt circle to the inside of the carton. Follow the clock works package instructions to insert the clock through the hole and to add the clock hands.

5. Cut a white felt oval and a smaller pink felt oval for the cow's face. Glue the white oval onto the top front of the carton, and the pink oval onto the white one. Cut out two small black dots for the cow's nostrils and glue them onto the pink nose.

Cut out a small pink tongue and glue it under the mouth.

6. For the ears, cut out two black ovals and two smaller pink ovals. Then, layer each pink oval over a black one and cut a straight line along one short edge. Fold each set of layered ear pieces in half and glue them to the top side edges of the carton.

7. Glue the googly eyes into place.

8. Cut out some white felt spots for the sides and top of the carton and glue in place.

PUNK ROCK PLANTER BOX

When grass grows out of top of this punky planter, the wacky face will have a punk hairdo suitable for styling. Mohawk or spikes, it's all up to you and your scissors!

MATERIALS

A half-gallon milk carton
12-inch x 18-inch (30.5-cm x 46-cm) sheet
  of orange craft foam
Scraps of colored craft foam (for the face)
A glue gun and glue sticks
A ruler, a pencil, and scissors
Potting soil
Grass seed

1. Measure and mark 4 inches (10 cm) up from each bottom corner of the carton. Use a ruler to draw a line between the marks and cut along the line to make a cube.

2. Measure, mark, and cut a piece of 4-inch x 18-inch (10-cm x 46-cm) orange craft foam.

3. Working on one side at a time, apply glue to each side of the carton and start wrapping the orange craft foam sheet around the carton to cover it completely.

4. Cut out a mouth, nose, eyes, and eyebrows from colored craft foam. Glue them onto the front of the planter box to form a face.

5. Fill the planter with potting soil. Sprinkle grass seed to cover the top of the soil. Water and place the planter in a sunny spot. Keep the soil moist while the grass is growing.

TWINKLE, TWINKLE LITTLE LAMP

With twinkle lights tucked inside, this little lamp will brighten any bedroom. To be on the safe side, make sure you use an LED light string because it will stay cool no matter how long it's shining. Also, make sure you don't leave the lamp on unattended.

MATERIALS

A half-gallon milk carton
Blue craft paint
Glitter glue
A 10-light LED mini light string
Scissors, a paintbrush, and a pen, nail,
  or thumbtack

1. Cut off the top of the milk carton around the top edge. The open end is the bottom of the lamp.
2. Paint the carton and let dry. Repeat two or three times until the carton is completely covered.
3. Using a pen, a nail, or a thumbtack, carefully poke small holes all over the carton.
4. With the glitter glue, draw on some swirls and dots. Let dry.
5. Cut a small notch in the bottom center of one carton side. Tuck the LED lights inside the carton, with the cord coming out through the notch. Plug in the lights and watch it glow.

Another Feathered Friends Feeder

Feed your bird buddies and watch them flock to your backyard. They'll be tweeting "Thank you!" with every peck. Just remember that you have to keep the feeder filled up with birdseed, or you'll have some sad and hungry little birdies.

MATERIALS

A half-gallon milk carton
12-inch-long (30.5-cm) thin wooden dowel
Thin wire or waterproof twine
Birdseed
A glue gun and glue sticks
A ruler, a pencil, a drinking glass with a wide
  opening, and scissors

1. Glue the spout of the carton shut. Let dry.

2. Measure and mark 2 inches (5 cm) from the bottom of one carton side. Place the drinking glass, open end down, on the carton side with the edge at the mark. Trace around the glass and then cut out the circle. Repeat on the opposite side of the carton.

3. Cut a small hole about 1 inch (2.5 cm) below each large hole. Poke the dowel through one small hole and out the other side.

4. Poke a very small hole at the top of the carton. Figure out where you want to hang the feeder and cut a piece of wire or twine that is long enough to hang it from there. Thread the wire or twine through the hole and tie it in a knot.

5. Fill the bottom 2 inches (5 cm) of the feeder with birdseed and hang it up.

My Favorite Pet Masks

You'll be ready for the next costume party with cute-as-a-button dog and cat masks.
If you want to take it to the next level, make some matching felt ears-pointy ears for the cat
and floppy ears for the dog-and glue them onto a hair band or a wide ribbon.

MATERIALS

A half-gallon milk carton for each mask
1 sheet each of orange, black, brown,
  pink, and gray felt
2 black pipe cleaners
1 pink pipe cleaner
2 pieces of thin ribbon or string
  (about 18 inches or 46 cm each)
  for each mask
A glue gun and glue sticks
A ruler, a pencil, and scissors

1. Measure and mark 2 inches (5 cm) up from each bottom corner of the carton. Use a ruler to draw a line between the marks and cut along the line to remove the carton bottom.

2. Measure, mark, and cut out a 9-inch × 9-inch (23-cm × 23-cm) piece of felt (brown for the dog mask and gray for the cat mask). Apply a thin layer of glue to the bottom of the carton and stick it to the center of the felt.

3. Cut the felt from the edge to each corner of the carton. Apply glue to the sides of the carton and press the felt up to cover the mask completely. Cut the felt along the corners to remove extra felt that extends beyond the carton. Then, apply a line of glue around the inside top of the carton and fold the felt edges over the carton edge and press them into the glue.

4. For the cat mask, cut two 4-inch (10-cm) pieces of pink pipe cleaner and bend each one into a J shape. Glue them onto the front of the mask to make the mouth as shown. Then, cut six 4-inch (10-cm) pieces of black pipe cleaner and glue them onto the front of the mask to make whiskers. Cut out a

pink triangle and round the points. Glue it over the whiskers.

5. For the dog mask, cut out a pink felt tongue and glue it onto the front of the mask. Cut two orange felt circles about two inches across. Glue them side-by-side above the tongue. Cut out a small black felt circle for the nose and glue it between the orange circles. Cut out six tiny dots and glue three onto each orange felt circle.

6. Carefully poke a hole through one side corner. Thread a piece of string or ribbon through the hole and tie a knot inside the mask. Repeat at the other side corner.

7. Poke three or four small air holes into each side of the mask.

Big Bubble Blower

Forget those puny bubbles your bubble wand makes! This blower will make much bigger
bubbles. It takes a little practice, and be sure to blow gently. When you have
a bubble on the end of the blower, keep your tongue on the end of the straw and
gently twirl the blower around to release the bubble.

MATERIALS

A one-quart milk carton
A drinking straw
½ cup (125 mL) liquid dish soap
2 teaspoons (10 mL) of sugar
Scissors
A jar
A small dish

1. Cut a 1-inch (2.5-cm) square hole in the center of the carton bottom.

2. Insert the straw into the spout so it is just inside the carton, and close the spout.

3. To make the bubble solution, mix 1 cup (250 mL) of water, ½ cup (125 mL) of liquid dish soap and 2 teaspoons (10 mL) of sugar in a jar.

4. Pour some bubble solution into a small dish and dip the bottom of the blower into it. Gently blow through the straw to make a bubble.

Breezy Day Wind Catcher

Tie this outside on a windy day and watch the streamers flutter and fly while you catch a breeze.

MATERIALS

A half-gallon milk carton
Pink craft paint
1 each of a pink, yellow, and green thin plastic
   tablecloth (from a party supply store)
24-inch (60-cm) piece of string or plastic lace
   for hanging
A glue gun and glue sticks
Scissors and a paintbrush

1. Cut off the top and bottom of the milk carton around the edges.

2. Paint the carton and let dry. Repeat two or three times until the carton is completely covered.

3. Cut four 1-inch-wide (2.5-cm) strips from the short edge of each tablecover.

4. Apply a line of glue to the inside of one edge of the carton. Stick three tablecover strips (one of each color) along the edge. Repeat three times to stick three strips to each inside carton edge.

5. Carefully poke a hole about an inch (2.5 cm) below one top carton edge. Repeat on the opposite side.

6. Thread the string in one hole and out the opposite hole. Tie the string around a bench or onto your porch and watch the streamers flow.

WOVEN WONDER PENCIL HOLDER

This colorful catchall will add style to any desk and keep you organized, too!
You can use two colors of plastic lace for vertical stripes, as shown,
or switch the colors partway up for a stripy extravaganza.

MATERIALS

A one-quart milk carton
2 spools of plastic lace,
  about 10 yards (9 m) each
A drinking glass
A ruler, a pencil, scissors, and tape

1. Measure and mark 5 inches up (12.5 cm) from each bottom corner of the carton. Use the ruler to draw a line between the marks and cut along the line to make a cube.

2. Cut down the seam of each corner edge from the top to the bottom corner. Push the carton sides down so they lie flat on the workspace. Measure, mark, and cut each side piece into three even strips, leaving the carton bottom uncut and the strips still attached to it. Then, cut a strip about ⅛-inch-wide (3 mm) from the right edge of each side strip.

3. To begin weaving, lay the carton piece with the white inside of the carton down. Tape one plastic lace end to one corner of the center square of the carton piece. Weave the lace over and under the carton strips, all the way around the carton, until you get back to where you started.

4. Tape the end of the second color of plastic lace over the first piece. Weave this piece under and over the carton strips, traveling in the same direction as the first piece of lace, but on the opposite side of each strip (so, where the first lace went over, the second one would go under). When you get back to the beginning, weave another row with the first lace.

5. Place a drinking glass in the center of the carton piece and gently lift the carton strips up. The glass

will create the shape of the pencil holder and make it easier to weave.

6. Continue weaving, alternating lace colors and the over/under pattern, until you are 1 inch (2.5 cm) from the top. Remove the glass. Cut the laces, leaving about 3 inches (7.5 cm) to tuck into the weaving below them.

7. Fold each carton strip over to the inside and tuck it under the woven laces to keep it in place.

THE BIG RIG

You'll be ready for the long haul with this tough tractor-trailer. Put your initials on the side or give your rig a name. Either way, you can load up your cargo and hit the road!

MATERIALS

2 one-quart milk cartons
Green metallic craft paint
Silver metallic craft paint
Three 4-inch (10-cm) dowels
1½-inch (4-cm) dowel
6 wooden circles, 1½ inches (4 cm) in diameter
Black craft paint
1 yellow peel-and-stick craft foam sheet
  (6 inches x 9 inches or about 16 cm x 23 cm)
Tinfoil
A glue gun and glue sticks
A ruler, a pencil, scissors, and a paintbrush

1. For the tractor, measure and mark 3 inches (7.5 cm) down from each top corner of one carton. Use a ruler to draw a line between the marks and cut along the line to remove the top.

2. For the trailer, cut the top off of the other milk carton.

3. Paint the tractor metallic green and let dry. Paint the trailer silver and let dry. Repeat two or three times until they are completely covered.

4. For the wheel axles, paint the dowel pieces and the wooden circles black and let dry.

5. Arrange the cartons so that they are lying on their sides, with the open ends facing toward each other. Measure, mark, and carefully poke a hole through the center of each side of the green tractor, about ½ inch (1.25 cm) up from the bottom edge. Repeat to poke holes about ½ inch (1.25 cm) up from the bottom edge of the silver trailer and about 1 inch (2.5 cm) in from the outer edges.

6. Slide the axles (the three 4-inch dowels) through the holes so that they are poking out of each side of the carton. Apply a generous blob of glue to the inside center of a wheel and glue it to the end of an axle, making sure it is centered. Hold it steady while it dries. Repeat to attach the other five wheels.

7. To add windows, cut two 1-inch × 1-inch (2.5-cm × 2.5-cm) tinfoil squares. Glue one square to each side of the tractor. For the windshield, cut a 1¼-inch × 2-inch (3-cm × 5-cm) tinfoil piece, and glue it to the front of the tractor. Let dry.

8. For the exhaust pipe, paint the 1½-inch (4-cm) dowel silver and let dry. Measure, mark, and carefully poke a hole through the top of the tractor—look at the drawing for the proper placement.

9. o attach the tractor and trailer, cut four ½-inch × 1-inch (1.25-cm × 2.5-cm) yellow foam pieces. Peel off the backing and stick two foam pieces to the top edges of the tractor and trailer, leaving a small gap. Stick the other two foam pieces to the bottom of the tractor and trailer, leaving the same small gap.

10. Cut out some letters from the yellow foam and stick them to the side of the trailer.

NOTE: For a Super Big Rig, use half-gallon containers. (Remember to adjust your measurements for the larger size.)

Ahoy Matey! Pirate Ship

Set sail, ye mateys, on a ship made for plundering. As the captain, you'll rule the seas, and if your crew mutinies, you can always add a plank for them to walk!

MATERIALS

A half-gallon milk carton
Black craft paint
2 sheets of black construction paper
1 sheet of white paper
1 small piece of red construction paper
4 drinking straws
A small paper cup
A glue gun and glue sticks
A paintbrush, a ruler, a pencil, scissors,
   and a black marker

1. Glue the spout of the carton closed. Paint all sides of the carton and drinking cup black and let dry. Repeat two or three times until they are completely covered.

2. For the center mast, cut one drinking straw in half. Fold about 3 inches (7.5 cm) of another drinking straw over and make a small vertical cut in the cen-ter of the fold. Unfold the straw. Slide one of the cut pieces of straw about halfway through the small cut in the other straw. Poke a small hole in the bottom of the drinking cup and slip the mast through the hole about 1 inch (2.5-cm). Apply a little glue around the hole and let dry.

3. For the front mast, cut a 6-inch × 8-inch (15.25-cm × 20.25-cm) piece of black paper. Cut out a 3-inch-diameter (7.5-cm) white paper circle. Cut out two small black paper circles and glue them onto the white circle for eyes. Draw a mouth, as shown, with a black marker. Cut two 1-inch × 5-inch (2.5-cm × 12.75-cm) white paper pieces with rounded ends and glue them to the sail in an X. Glue the skull on top of the X. Let dry.

4. To add the sail to the front mask, cut a small slot

near the top center of each short side of the sail. Slip a straw through the two slots, keeping the paper curved as shown. Apply a little glue at the back of the sail near each slot to keep the sail in place. Hold while drying.

5. Cut a small, long triangle from the red paper. Apply glue to the top of the other cut straw piece and wrap the red flag end around it. Let dry. Pinch the end of this straw and slip it into the top of the front mast.

6. For the back mast, cut a 3½-inch × 4½-inch (9-cm × 11.5-cm) piece of black paper. Cut a small slot near the top center of each long side. Slip the remaining straw through the two slots, keeping the paper curved and near one end of the straw. Glue in place as in step 3. Then, cut a 5-inch × 6-inch (12.75-cm × 15.25-cm) piece of black paper. Repeat to cut slots and glue it below the smaller sail. Let dry.

7. Lay the milk carton on its side, with the top spout edge vertical. Apply a generous blob of glue to the center top of the carton. Put the center mast into the glue and hold it upright until it dries. Repeat to glue the front and back masts about 1½ (4 cm) inches from each end.

CITYSCAPE PLAY MAT

Grab your mini cars and hit the streets for some urban adventures. Once you've got
the streets and buildings set up, why not add some street signs made from drinking straws
and colored paper, and some trees and grass made from green tissue paper
and paper towel rolls? The sky's the limit in this big city.

MATERIALS

1 piece of green foam core board (20 inches ×
  30 inches or about 50 cm × 76 cm)
Milk cartons in several sizes
Black and white craft paint, plus some colors for
  the buildings
A glue gun and glue sticks
A ruler, a pencil, scissors, a paintbrush, and a
  medium black marker

1. For the main street, measure and draw a line 6
   inches (15.25 cm) from one long edge of the board.
   Draw another line 5 inches (12.75 cm) over from
   the first line. For one side street, start 10 inches
   (25.5 cm) from one short edge and measure and
   draw a line from the long edge to the main street.
   Draw another line 5 inches (12.75 cm) over from
   this line. Repeat to add another side street to the
   other side of the main street.

2. Paint the streets black between the lines you drew
   in step 1. Let dry. Paint white dotted lines down the
   center of each street.

3. Glue each of the milk carton tops closed.

4. Cut some of the milk cartons into different sizes,
   and leave some of them uncut. Paint each carton
   and let dry. Repeat to completely cover each carton.

5. With the black marker, decorate each building with
   windows, doors, shop signs and any other details
   you like.

6. Arrange the buildings along the streets and glue the
   bottom of each to the board. Let dry. Or, you can
   leave the buildings unglued so that you can move
   them around.

GALAXY ALEX THE ROBOT

Take a trip to the outer limits of space with a best 'bot pal. You can decorate it as shown or
rummage through the tool box and add your own style with different hardware bits.

MATERIALS

A half-gallon milk carton
A one-quart milk carton
A cardboard tube from inside
  a toilet paper roll
Silver craft paint
4-inch (10-cm) piece of red pipe cleaner
Red, green, and orange craft foam
2 large googly eyes
4 metal washers
5 metal nuts
A glue gun and glue sticks
A ruler, a pencil, scissors,
  and a paintbrush

1. For the body, cut off the top of the half-gallon milk carton around the top edge.

2. For the head, measure and mark 2 inches (5 cm) up from each bottom corner of the one-quart carton. Use a ruler to draw a line between the marks and cut along the line to make a cube.

3. With the open ends down, glue the head to the body. Let dry.

4. For the legs, cut the cardboard tube in half to make two shorter tubes. Fold one tube flat, and then cut halfway down each folded edge. Unfold the tube and slide the cut lines of the tube onto the bottom of the body. Repeat with the other tube. Arrange the legs so the robot stands on its own, and then apply some glue to the inside of the carton to glue the legs in place.

5. Paint the robot silver and let dry. Repeat two or three times until the robot is completely covered.

6. Wrap the pipe cleaner around your finger to make a spiral. Glue one end to the top of the head.

7. Glue the googly eyes to the front of the head. Glue

a metal nut to each side of the head for ears. Cut a zigzag mouth out of red foam and glue it below the eyes.

8. Glue three metal washers in a line at the top of the body. Measure and cut a 2-inch × 2-inch (5-cm × 5-cm) green foam square and glue it below the washers. Cut a smaller orange foam square and glue it over the green one. Glue a metal washer in the middle of the orange square. Glue three metal washers below the foam. Let dry.

9. For the arms, cut two 1½-inch × 3½-inch (4-cm × 9-cm) red foam rectangles. Cut slits at one end of each for the fingers and thumb. Glue the arms to the sides of the robot.

DANGEROUS DINOSAUR

Sixty-five million years ago there were dinosaurs almost as fierce as this one.

Why not make a second dino in another color so they can battle for the rule of the Earth?

MATERIALS

A one-quart milk carton
I egg cup from a cardboard egg carton
Green craft paint
2 green peel-and-stick craft foam sheets
  (6 inches x 9 inches or, about 15.25 cm x
  23 cm)
2 large googly eyes
A glue gun and glue sticks
A ruler, a pencil, scissors, and a paintbrush

1. Cut off the top of the milk carton around the top edge.

2. For the mouth, cut the egg cup in half to make two even pieces. Then, cut a zigzag edge along the cut edges to make teeth.

3. With the open carton end down, glue the two mouth pieces near the top of one carton side.

4. Paint the carton green. Let dry and repeat two or three times to cover it completely.

5. Peel the backing from the foam sheets and stick them together evenly.

6. Cut a 1-inch x 9-inch (2.5-cm x 23-cm) piece of foam. Cut a zigzag along one edge and then glue it along the center of the back of the dinosaur.

7. Cut a boot shape from the foam that is about 3½ inches (9 cm) high and about 2 inches (5 cm) wide across the foot. Cut a zigzag edge along the bottom. Repeat to make a second foot. Glue one foot to the center bottom of each side of the carton.

8. For the arms, cut a ¾-inch x 3-inch (2-cm x 7.5-cm) piece of foam and cut a zigzag along one short edge. Repeat to make a second arm. Glue one arm to each side of the carton.

9. Glue two googly eyes above the mouth.

COURAGEOUS KNIGHT CROWN

Don this crown and brandish your sword, and you'll be ready for
fierce battles and dangerous quests. Dragons beware!

MATERIALS

A half-gallon milk carton
Silver craft paint
Metal studs
Plastic jewels
A glue gun and glue sticks
24-inch (60 cm) piece of thin ribbon
  or string
A ruler, a pencil, scissors, a dinner plate,
  and a paintbrush

1. Open the top of the milk carton completely. Then, cut down one side corner edge. Cut the carton bottom off along the bottom edges and open the carton flat.

2. Measure and make a few marks 3½ inches (9 cm) up from the bottom edge of the carton. Draw a line between the marks and cut along the line.

3. Measure and make a mark 2 inches (5 cm) up from each side corner. Make another mark at the center of the top edge of the carton piece.

4. Lay the dinner plate upside down along the top edge of the carton piece, with one edge of the plate at the center mark and the other edge at one of the side marks you made in step 3. Trace along the edge of the plate to make a curved line between these points. Repeat on the other side of the carton piece.

5. Cut along the curved lines.

6. Paint the blank side of the crown with silver paint. Let dry and then repeat.

7. Add metal studs along the edges of the crown by gently pressing the points through from the front to

the back. Turn the crown over and use blunt scissor ends or a flat screwdriver to press the stud points down flat.

8. Glue on a few plastic jewels.

9. Poke a small hole at each side edge. Cut the ribbon in half. Slip one ribbon end through a hole and make a knot at the back of the crown. Repeat with the other ribbon and the other hole.

SECRET STORAGE ROCKET

Blast off to the Milky Way in a rocket made for distant galaxies. And this rocket holds a secret-inside the little door is a great place to stash your most valuable treasures.

MATERIALS

A half-gallon milk carton
Tinfoil
11-inch x 18-inch (28-cm x 46-cm) sheet of
  orange craft foam
Small pieces of yellow, red, and green
  craft foam
White craft glue
A glue gun and glue sticks
Scissors, a ruler, a pencil, scissors, a paintbrush,
  and a plate that is about 8 inches (20.25 cm)
  in diameter

1. Cut off the top of the milk carton around the top edge.

2. Tear off a 14-inch-long (35.5 cm) piece of tinfoil. Lay it shiny-side-down onto a work surface. With a paintbrush, apply a thin layer of white craft glue to all four carton sides. Lay the carton onto the tinfoil and wrap the foil around it, smoothing as you go. Apply some extra glue to the overlapped edges to stick them down. Apply glue and tuck the open foil edges over the carton top and bottom. Allow to dry overnight.

3. Lay the plate onto the orange foam sheet and trace around the edges. Cut out the foam circle. Then, measure and draw a line dividing the circle in half. Cut along the line from one edge to the circle center.

4. Fold the cut circle edges around, overlapping each other to make a cone shape that is just a little bigger than the top of the carton. Glue the cone edges together. With the glue gun, glue the cone to the top of the carton.

5. To make the fins, measure, mark, and cut two 2-inch

× 3-inch (5-cm × 7.5-cm) orange foam pieces. Glue the pieces together evenly. Repeat three more times. Let dry.

6. Starting at one corner of a fin, measure and make a mark 2 inches (5 cm) along the long edge, and then 1 inch (2.5 cm) along the short edge. Draw a diagonal line between the points. At the opposite corner, measure and make a mark 1 inch (2.5 cm) along both the short and long edges. Draw a diagonal line between these points. Cut along the two lines. Use this fin as a template to cut the other three fins into the same shape.

7. Apply a thin line of glue from the glue gun along a long, straight edge of one fin and stick to the bottom corner edge of the carton. Let dry. Repeat to stick one fin to each carton corner edge.

8. To cut the door, measure and mark a 2½-inch × 3-inch (6.25-cm × 7.5-cm) rectangle in the center of one of the rocket. Cut along three of the four lines to open the door. Glue one of the leftover triangles you cut from the fins to the front of the door as a handle. Let dry.

9. Cut one small circle each from the yellow, red, and green foam. Glue them in a row above the door.

FUNKY FLOWER VASE

Totally waterproof and totally adorable, too, all this colorful vase needs is a bunch of daisies.

No fresh flowers? Why not make some matching tissue paper flowers instead?

MATERIALS

A one-quart milk carton
White craft paint
Colored tissue paper
White craft glue or Mod Podge
Scissors and a paintbrush

1. Cut off the top of the milk carton around the top edge.

2. Paint the carton and let dry. Repeat two or three times until the carton is completely covered.

3. Cut strips of tissue paper that are about 1 inch (2.5 cm) wide and at least 12 inches (30.5 cm) long.

4. Starting at the bottom, apply a thin coat of glue around the carton. Press a strip of tissue paper onto the glue, overlapping the ends at the back. Continue adding strips, overlapping them a little, until the entire vase is covered. Let dry.

5. Apply a thin coat of glue over the entire vase. Let dry.

Darling Dollhouse

Even the tiniest dolls need a place to live. Create the cutest living space for them, and use the leftover milk carton pieces to cut out some simple furniture. Decorate their rooms with bits of felt, craft foam, and decorative paper scraps, and you can even add a craft foam garden. The possibilities are endless!

MATERIALS

2 half-gallon milk cartons
Craft paint in a few colors
A glue gun and glue sticks
Scissors, a ruler, a pencil, and a paintbrush
Felt, craft foam and decorative paper to
  decorate

1. Carefully cut the front from each carton along the side and top edges, leaving the carton top uncut. Set aside one of the carton fronts for the second storey floors.

2. Glue the cartons together with the open sides facing the same way. Let dry.

3. Measure, mark, and draw a line dividing the carton front you set aside in step 1 in half from top to bottom. Cut along the line just a little more than halfway. Cut another line about ⅛-inch (3-mm) over from the first, and then remove the thin strip of carton to make a narrow slit.

4. Repeat step 3 on the inside wall of the dollhouse. With the white side of the carton front up, slide the two slits together. Apply a line of glue along the underside edges of the floors to stick them to the dollhouse walls. Let dry.

5. Paint the outside of the dollhouse. Let dry and repeat. Paint the roof a different color. Let dry and repeat.

6. Decorate with some furniture, felt rugs, wallpaper, or whatever else you like.

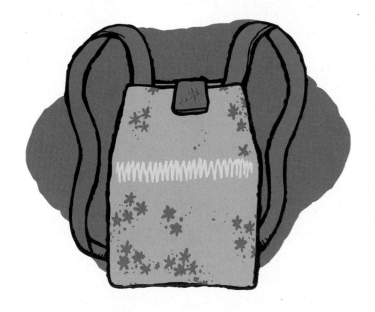

Posh Party Purse

Tote your necessities in a pretty little purse that's ready to party. Make one to match every one of your fancy outfits and you'll always be ready for the next big event.

MATERIALS

A half-gallon milk carton
9-inch x 18-inch (23 cm x 46 cm)
  piece of fabric
39-inch-long (1 meter) piece of ribbon
A small piece of Velcro
A glue gun and glue sticks
A pencil, a ruler, and scissors

1. Measure and mark 6 inches (15.25 cm) up from each bottom corner of the carton. Draw a line between the marks and cut along the line to make a cube.

2. Lay the carton onto the back side of the fabric with the open carton end about 1 inch (2.5 cm) below one long edge. Fold one short edge of the fabric over and glue the edge onto the carton. Fold the second short edge over, wrapping the fabric around the carton and, tucking the cut edge under, glue the second edge over the first. Let dry.

3. Apply a line of glue along the inside top edge of the carton. Fold the fabric edges over to the inside. Let dry.

4. On the bottom, fold the fabric as you would wrap the ends of a present, gluing as you go. Let dry. Gently bend the front and back edges of the purse together, folding in the sides.

5. For the handles, measure and cut two 18-inch (46-cm) pieces of ribbon. Glue one 18-inch (46-cm) ribbon end to the inside top left edge of the purse and the other end to the inside top right edge. Repeat with the other 18-inch (46-cm) ribbon on the other side of the purse. Let dry.

6. For the closure, apply a dab of glue to each end of the remaining 3-inch (8 cm) piece of ribbon, and then fold over about ½ inch (1.25 cm) of the ends and press into the glue. Glue one ribbon end about 1 inch (2.5 cm) below the top center of the back of the purse. Glue one half of the Velcro piece to the inside of the other end of the ribbon. Glue the second half of the Velcro piece just below the top center of the front of the purse. Squeeze the purse closed and fasten the Velcro pieces together.

Bedazzling Jewelry Box

Keep your best baubles in a jeweled box fit for a queen.
After all, your pretty jewelry deserves a pretty place to be.

MATERIALS

A half-gallon milk carton
4 round wooden beads
Pink craft paint
A piece of pink felt
Plastic jewels
A small peel-and-stick Velcro circle
A glue gun and glue sticks
A ruler, a pencil, scissors, and
  a paintbrush

1. Measure and mark 3 inches (7.5 cm) up from three bottom corners of the carton. Draw a line between the marks and cut along the line, leaving the fourth side uncut.

2. Cut along the side and top edges of the fourth side for the lid. Fold the lid down over the top of the box, and then fold the front edge over to make a front flap.

3. Glue one wooden bead to each bottom corner of the box.

4. Paint the outside of the box pink. Let dry and repeat two or three times to cover it completely.

5. Measure, mark, and cut out pink felt pieces to fit the sides and bottom inside the box. Glue them in place and let dry.

6. Decorate the outside of the box by gluing on plastic jewels.

7. Stick one half of the Velcro circle to the inside flap of the lid. Stick the other Velcro half to the center top of the front panel.

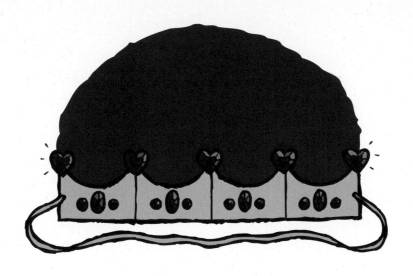

Pretty Princess Tiara

Dash off to the ball in a dazzling crown suitable for any aspiring princess.
Let's hope Prince Charming is at the ball, too!

MATERIALS

A half-gallon milk carton
Gold craft paint
Plastic jewels
24-inch (60-cm) piece of thin ribbon
A glue gun and glue sticks
Ruler, pencil, scissors, a mug, a paintbrush

1. Open the top of the milk carton completely. Then, cut down one side corner edge. Cut the carton bottom off along the bottom edges and open the carton flat.

2. Measure and make a few marks 3½ inches (9 cm) up from the bottom edge of the carton. Draw a line between the marks and cut along the line.

3. Measure and mark the center of the top edge of the carton piece. Then, measure and make a mark halfway between the center point and each side edge.

4. Lay the mug upside down along the top edge of the carton piece, with one edge of the mug at one top corner and the other edge at the closest mark you made in step 3. Trace along the edge of the mug to make a curved line between these points. Repeat between each of the marks from step 3.

5. Cut along the curved lines. If necessary, trim the peaks of the crown so they aren't too tall.

6. Paint the blank side of the crown with gold paint. Let dry and then repeat.

7. Glue plastic jewels onto the crown as shown or in a design that you like.

8. Poke a small hole at each side edge. Cut the ribbon in half. Slip one ribbon end through a hole and make a knot at the back of the crown. Repeat with the other piece of ribbon and the other hole.

GORGEOUS GIFT BOX

Tuck a gift inside this beautiful box, and you'll be giving two gifts in one!
Once the present is opened, the box will be a perfectly pretty way
to store jewelry or hair doo-dads on a dresser.

MATERIALS

A half-gallon milk carton
A piece of decorative or wrapping paper, about
  11 inches x 18 inches (28 cm x 46 cm)
24-inch (60-cm) piece of ribbon
A ruler, a pencil, scissors, white craft glue or
  Mod Podge, a single-hole punch

1. Measure and mark 3 inches (7.5 cm) up from three bottom corners of the carton. Draw a line between the marks and cut along the line, leaving the fourth side uncut.

2. Cut along the side and top edges of the fourth side to make the lid. Fold the lid down over the top of the box, and then fold the front edge over to make a front flap.

3. Measure, mark, and cut out a 4-inch x 5-inch (10-cm x 12.75-cm) piece of decorative paper. Apply a thin coat of glue to the lid of the box and smooth the paper over it, overlapping the front and back edges.

4. Measure, mark and cut out a 3-inch x 18-inch (7.5-cm x 46-cm) piece of decorative paper. Starting at the center of the back of the box, apply a thin coat of glue and smooth the paper over it. Continue around all four sides of the box, overlapping the paper at the back of the box. Let dry.

5. Punch a hole in each side of the box, about 1 inch (2.5 cm) below the top and centered left to right. Cut the ribbon in half and thread one piece through one hole, tying a knot on the inside of the box. Repeat with the other ribbon. Pop a gift inside the box, close the lid, and tie a bow on top.

Four Friends Picture Frame Cube

Slip a picture into each of the four sides of this cute cube, and you'll have a spot for each of your best pals. Or choose craft foam in the colors of your sports team, and you can cheer for your teammates all year long.

MATERIALS

A half-gallon milk carton
2 sheets of craft foam
  (8½ inches × 11 inches or, about 21.5 cm
  × 28 cm each)
A glue gun and glue sticks
A ruler, a pencil, and scissors

1. Measure and mark 3¾ inches (9.5 cm) up from each bottom corner of the carton. Draw a line between the marks and cut along the line to make a cube.

2. Measure and cut five 3¾-inch × 3¾-inch (9.5-cm × 9.5-cm) foam squares.

3. Glue one foam square to the bottom of the carton. This is the top of the picture frame cube.

4. Measure and cut the center out of the other four foam squares, leaving a ¾-inch (2-cm) border.

5. Starting on one side of the cube, apply glue to three sides of a foam frame and glue it to one side of the cube, with the unglued edge at the top. Repeat for the other three sides. Pop in your pictures.